The Smell Of Rain

Dr. Vaidehi Borkar

BookLeaf Publishing

India | USA | UK

Made with ❤ on the BookLeaf Publishing Platform
www.bookleafpub.in
www.bookleafpub.com

Dedication

To my parents,
Prasanna and Rutuja.

In the fragrance of memories, I offer this, my first book, 'The Smell of Rain', as a tribute to your unwavering love and guidance. Your presence in my life has been a sanctuary, nurturing my dreams and shaping my soul. May these words, like the scent of rain, evoke the beauty and wonder of life and remind you of the love and gratitude that fills my heart.

With deepest affection,
Vaidehi.

Preface

"I want to be defined by the things that I love,
not the things I hate,
not the things I'm afraid of,
or the things that haunt me in the middle of the night.

I think that you are what you love."

In the pages that follow, I invite you to embark on a
journey of self-discovery, couragee, and resilience.
Through a tapestry of poetry, I share my experiences and
the lessons that have shaped me. This book is a
testament to the transformative power of courage, hope,
and the human spirit.

There is room for all of you here, and it is possible to
believe in starlit dreams. To the rare, beautiful human
beings who change our lives forever, I offer these words:
"You are not the legacy of life's fragile moments, but the
testament of your unyielding spirit. You are the sum of
all that you refused to surrender, the essence of what
remains unbroken."

To all those who have ever been told they are too much -

the ones who are too loud, too emotional, too bold, and the quiet ones with stories swirling in their minds - I see you. To those who have known hurt, but chose to hope, to forgive, to heal, and to rise above, you are beacons of resilience, proof that light will always prevail. And to the stargazers, the dreamers, the wishers, may your aspirations be the guiding stars that illuminate your journey. You are enough, you are seen, you are loved.

"The most beautiful people we have known are those who have known defeat, known suffering, known struggle, known loss, and have found their way out of the depths. These persons have an appreciation, a sensitivity, and an understanding of life that fills them with compassion, gentleness, and a deep loving concern. Beautiful people do not just happen."

To each one of you who picks up "The Smell of Rain," I wish you the best: good books, travel, thunder, sunshine, rainy days, and hot chocolate.

May these words be a reminder that courage, hope, and resilience can guide us through life's journey.

With love always,
Vaidehi

Acknowledgements

"To give thanks in solitude is enough. Thanksgiving has wings and goes where it must go. Your prayer knows much more about it than you do." ~ Victor Hugo.

Sorry, Victor Hugo, I don't agree. I want to thank people personally.

I put my thanks at the front because it gives my readers an idea of how the book has grown and who's contributed, and how and why.

First and foremost: My father, Dr. Prasanna Borkar. My father, my ever-patient father, who has always been present in every aspect of my life, in operating rooms and off-operating rooms. My father has taught me everything from administering an injection to administrating decision-making. My father has always been my pillar of strength and my best friend. Thank you for being my constant light, the light of my life. For holding my hand tightly, even when it gets sweaty. No one means more to me than you.

My Mother, Dr. Rutuja Borkar, the brightest place of all. My mother, who knows the chapters of my life I have left unsaid. Whose constant warmth and companionship, I can never repay. My mother, who is my best friend has been the constant source of wind under my wings. My mother, who carries skies in her eyes and grace like flowers in her ways. Who has taught me lessons beyond textbooks. My life starts with your heartbeats.

My younger brother, Shaunmukh. There are places in the heart you don't even know exist until you love a child. In my life, that child has been my younger brother.

Through my first book, The Smell of Rain, I pay rich tributes to my dadaji, late Dr. Vasant Borkar, and my nanaji, late Mr. Sadashio Meshram.

My dadaji, Dr. Vasant Borkar who bestowed upon me the great art of medicine and surgery, also instilled in me a fond love of literature, which has been passed down through him. My earliest memories with you include me attempting to read a Stephen Covey with you. If it was not for a childhood spent under the vast canopy of your immense collection of books, I wouldn't be here. I treasure the books once owned by you, with your inscriptions, closest to my heart.

My nanaji, Mr. Sadashio Mesharam who nurtured in me a love for plants and animals, taught me the values of love, compassion, and the great virtues of life. You taught me the value of selflessness, showing me how to put others first, give with kindness, and serve with compassion. I cherish the memories of our time together, watering your plants and nurturing life. Every poem about a tree in my book serves as a fond reminder of you.

Every copy of this book, now and forever, will bear your names, ensuring your legacy lives on through me.

Thank you to all the people I've met in my travels over the years- some of whom I kept in touch with, some of whom I put into this book, and some of whom have changed the trajectory of my life. Without you, I would not be here now, writing these words.

To all the individuals I have had the opportunity to lead, be led by, or watch their leadership from afar, I want to say thank you for being the inspiration and foundation. Having an idea and turning it into a book is as hard as it sounds. The experience is both internally challenging and rewarding. I especially want to thank all the individuals who helped make this happen. Thanks to everyone on the Bookleaf Publications team who helped me so much.

To anyone who has ever found strength in the shadows.
For anyone who has ever wanted to give up
but chose to keep going
to keep trying
to keep hoping
to keep surviving:
This book is for us.

1. The Smell of Rain

Scents of memory, whispers of the past
Echoes of moments that forever last
A fragrance wafts, and suddenly I'm there
In a bygone era, with love and care

The perfume of roses, a grandmother's gentle touch
Fresh-cut grass, summers of childhood's rush
The wood smoke of winters, fireside tales and dreams
Each scent a time machine, transporting heart and
themes

The smell of rain, a melancholy sigh
Petrichor's sweet whisper, a nostalgic goodbye
To memories of laughter, of love and of tears
Washed clean by the rain, through all the passing years

In the fragrance of old books, wisdom and knowledge
sleep
In the aroma of freshly baked bread, memories softly
creep

Each whiff a journey, through time and space and heart
Fragrances, the closest we'll come, to never being apart.

2. A Love Letter to Life

Bake bread, sit under willow's sway
Gaze at stars, on a celestial day
Survive life's storms, and find peaceful nest
In second-hand stores, discover love that's been blessed

Buy something worn, yet precious and true
A reminder of souls who forever shine through
Write letters old-school, with pen and paper dear
To oneself, to God, to hearts that need to hear

Bury regret, plant a tree in its place
Carve pain in sand, watch it wash away with grace
Read of heaven's promise, or growth's gentle art
Take notes, and build a fire that warms the heart

Remember bravery, be gentle on your soul
Find peace in quiet moments, a heart made whole
For in these stillnesses, you will find a peaceful nest
A sense of purpose, a heart that's truly blessed.

3. You are the Stories you Tell

The tales you whisper, the legends you share
Are the threads that weave, the fabric of you there
In every word, a piece of your soul takes flight
A glimpse of your heart, a shard of your light

The scent of rain on pavement, a memory unfolds
Of laughter and tears, of stories yet untold
The petrichor's sweet whisper, a nostalgic sigh
Echoes of moments, that forever will lie

You are the stories, of love and of loss
Of every laughter, and every tender cross
You are the whispers, of wisdom and of might
A living, breathing narrative, that shines with delight

So tell your stories, let your voice be heard
For in the tales you share, your true self is stirred
And as you speak, your heart beats strong and free
A symphony of stories, that is the melody of you and we.

4. Stardust and Smiles

If every soul you've touched were to shine,
A constellation of love would be divine.
The strangers you've helped, the hearts you've made
bright,
Would light up the world, on a celestial night.

If every laugh you've shared, every tear you've dried,
Were to leave a sparkle, the world would be glorified.
The lives you've inspired, the dreams you've made real,
Would create a tapestry, of love that would reveal.

You are a thread, in a beautiful design,
A shining star, that twinkles like a diamond mine.
Your impact is grand, your love is pure and bright,
You are a treasure, a precious gem, a guiding light.

So let your heart be proud, your spirit aglow,
For you are a shining star, in a world that needs to know.
Keep on sparkling, keep on shining your light,
And know that you are making, a beautiful sight.

5. Windows of Hope

Keep looking out the window,
To the part of the road,
Where the light pours in,
and hope is made.

For that is where you'll be reminded,
Again and again, no matter the test,
These shadows cannot hold you,
you are blessed.

Their darkness may descend,
but it will not stay,
For you are a child of light,
and you will find your way.

So gaze out at the horizon,
where the sun meets the sky,
And remember that you are stronger,
than the shadows that pass by.

You are a beacon of hope,
a shining light in the night,
And no matter what happens,
you will emerge, radiant and bright.

6. October

Soft moss beneath my feet, a gentle caress,
As I wander through forests, where memories rest.
Forgotten paths unfold, like a tale of old,
Where fireflies dance, in a golden glow, young and bold.

Their twinkling lights, like tiny lanterns bright,
Lead me through the trees, on this autumnal night.
White laundry flutters, like a ghostly sigh,
As the breeze whispers secrets, as the trees lean by.

Somewhere below, a brook flows smooth and deep,
Like honey spilling from a pot, its sweetness to keep.
The sky dims slowly, as the cicadas begin to sing,
Their melodic hum, a lullaby, that makes my heart take
wing.

In this enchanted moment, my heart is alive with feeling,
As the beauty of October, my soul is gently revealing.
A sense of peace settles, like a soft blanket on the
ground,

As I breathe in the magic, of this autumnal sound.

7. My Mother- an Infectious Delight

Her eyes would light up,
like stars in the night,
And draw you in,
with a warm and inviting light.

A giggle so infectious,
it would spread like a flame,
And crawl across your skin,
leaving a happy, tingling claim.

Her laughter was contagious,
a joyous, sparkling sound,
That would wrap around your heart,
and spin you around.

It was a melody so sweet,
that it would make you smile,
And draw you in, with a warmth,
that would stay with you awhile.

With every chuckle,
her eyes would crinkle at the sides,
And her smile would grow wider,
like a sunrise in the skies.

Her joy was a magnet,
that would pull you in with ease,
And make you feel like you're home,
in a warm and cozy breeze.

In her presence,
your heart would feel lighter and free,
And her infectious laughter,
would be the key.

So let her giggle wrap around you,
like a warm and fuzzy hug,
And let her joyous laughter,
fill your heart with love.

8. Beyond You

Be close to things that make you feel humble and new,
Hills, seas, oceans, skies, stars, shining true.
For in their grandeur, we find our place,
A sense of perspective, a gentle, quiet space.

Love and dreams, they whisper low,
Of the beauty in being part of something greater to
know.
The first step to greatness, is to acknowledge our part,
To recognize the vastness, of the universe's loving heart.

So let's not be afraid, to feel the weight,
Of our own humanity, in the grand tapestry's fate.
For in embracing it, we find the courage to roam,
And to grow, to expand, to become our truest home.

Now go, grow, and let your spirit soar,
For in the vastness, lies a beauty to explore.
And though we may be one part, our hearts can be

grand,
And our dreams, they can take us, to the farthest land.

9. The Story of Courage

It's not the absence of fear that makes us bold,
But the willingness to act, despite the heart's cold.
Courage is the trembling, the stuttering start,
The uncertainty that grips, but doesn't capture the heart.

It's the shaking knees, the dry mouth's plight,
The choking on words, that refuse to take flight.
But still we step forward, into the unknown night,
And find our voice, our strength, in the morning's first
light.

Courage is not fearlessness, but the determination to try,
To push beyond the comfort zone, and reach for the sky.
It's the resilience of the heart, the refusal to give in,
The persistence of the soul, that finds a way to begin.

So let us not be fooled, by the bravado and the boast,
For true courage lies in vulnerability, and the willingness
to be toast.
It's the quiet strength, the inner voice, that whispers "go",

And the heart that beats with courage, in the face of the unknown.

15

10. Summertime Awakening

As sunshine spills, and leaves burst forth,
On trees that stretch, with vibrant birth,
Like scenes in fast-motion, growth unfolds,
A new beginning stirs, young and bold.

In summer's warmth, I feel it rise,
A familiar sense, that opens wide my eyes,
A conviction strong, that life starts anew,
A chance to rediscover, all that's true.

The world awakens, fresh and bright,
A canvas waiting, for life's vibrant light,
The trees regain their vibrancy and hue,
As summer's promise, brings life anew.

In this season's birth, I find my own,
A chance to start again, to make it known,
That life's beginnings are not just one,
But many moments, when love and hope are won.

11. The Flower of Connection

Why is it that when the story ends,
We begin to feel it all,
and the emotions transcend?
The laughter, the tears, the joy and the pain,
All surface at once,
like a heart that's about to break in vain.

But then, a simple flower, can change it all,
A small gesture of kindness,
can make another soul stand tall.
A smile, a word, a listening ear,
Can be the catalyst,
for a heart that's been holding back tears.

It's the human connection, that we all crave,
A sense of belonging,
a feeling that we're not alone in this wave.
A simple flower, can be the start,

Of a beautiful friendship, that's been waiting in the
heart.

12. Remember when?

Days of happiness, laughter free,
Chocolate and disaster, a memory to be.
Oh, those good old days, so pure and bright,
A nostalgic whisper, on a summer's night.

Rainy days and dance, a joyful sound,
Scribbling on walls, without a care around.
Oh, those good old days, so wild and free,
A childhood magic, that's meant to be.

Miles of running, without a single care,
Twisted slides and laughter, that filled the air.
Oh, those good old days, so full of glee,
A youthful energy, that's hard to see.

Climbing trees and dancing, on sun-kissed streets,
A carefree spirit, that skipped to the beat.
Oh, that good old life, so simple and true,
A nostalgic longing, that forever shines through.

13. A Wildflower Heart

May your heart be like a wildflower,
Resilient and strong, in every hour.
May it rise again, after being worn,
And weather life's storms, with a spirit reborn.

May it flourish in broken places,
And find a way, through life's troubled spaces.
May its beauty shine, like a beacon bright,
And guide you forward, through the darkest night.

May your heart be tough, yet gentle as can be,
A refuge for hope, and a heaven for glee.
May it bloom forever, in the garden of your soul,
A wildflower heart, that forever makes you whole.

14. The Joy of Simple Things

Every morning, every evening's pace,
I walk past trees and buildings in this place,
Yet each time feels different, a unique delight,
A sense of wonder that shines with new light.

The lissome trees, they sway and dance with glee,
Their leaves rustling softly, a symphony to me,
The breeze whispers secrets, as I wander by,
And I drink in the beauty, with a heart full of sighs.

Oh, may I never tire, of this wondrous sight,
May my heart remain open, to the beauty that's in sight,
May I never grow up, to be someone who can't see,
The small, beautiful things, that bring joy to you and me.

For in these trees and breezes, I find peaceful rest,
A sense of connection, to the world's gentle best,
So let me walk this path, with heart and soul awake,
And may the beauty of life, forever be my heart's sake.

15. Heartfelt

Sometimes people are beautiful, not in face,
But in truth and honesty that time and space,
Cannot erase, but only make more clear,
A beauty that's not skin-deep, but casts out fear.

A woman's plainness fades from sight,
When kindness, compassion, and love shine bright,
For beauty is not just a physical guise,
But a reflection of the heart's deep surprise.

We focus on looks, but they soon fade away,
As we get to know someone, day by day,
Their inner beauty shines, like a beacon bright,
Illuminating all, with its warm and gentle light.

There's nothing more beautiful, than a heart that cares,
That goes out of its way, to show it truly shares,
In the joy and the pain, of those around,
A beauty that's not just seen, but profoundly found.

16. Rakhi

She danced with life,
and life entwined,
A celestial ballet,
with hearts and souls aligned.

The universe, aglow, with vibrant,
pulsing light,
Reflected her essence,
in all its beauty and might.

In dewy mornings,
star-studded midnight skies,
Colors of sunrise,
in her presence, rise.

Incandescent glow,
that shines like a beacon bright,
Illuminating all, with pure,
radiant delight.

The world, in splendor,
shone with fervent, ardent zeal,
Hoping to catch her eye,
and make her heart reveal.

For in her presence,
life's vibrant pulse beats strong and free,
A symphony of joy,
that echoes wild and beautifully.

17. Whispers from the Wild

In ancient woods, where whispers roam,
A language echoed, that I'd always known.
A distant lullaby, from the womb of the earth,
A soothing melody, of peace and rebirth.

The forest spoke to my soul, in a gentle, sweet tone,
A reminder of solace, that I'd long known as home.
In the silence, I heard the whispers of old,
A symphony of wisdom, that only nature can hold.

The trees, like sentinels, stood guard with gentle might,
Their leaves, a soft rustling, a lullaby through the night.
The wind, a gentle caress, that soothed my soul's dark
place,
And in the stillness, I found a sense of peace, a warm,
safe space.

In this sanctuary, I found my heart's true home,
A place where love and wisdom, forever roam.
The forest's lullaby, a song that I'd always known,

Echoed deep within me, and made my spirit whole.

18. My father- The joy of my life

A man of depth, of substance and might,
The one I grew up dreaming of, day and night.
The one I fall in love with, every single day,
My father, my hero, in every single way.

He gives me perspective, a new point of view,
Makes the ordinary, extraordinary and true.
With words that weave magic, he makes my heart sing,
And in his presence,my life takes wing.

He makes me wonder, at life's little charms,
And adds wonder to my life, dispelling all alarms.
He is the life of my life, my guiding light,
The most amazing wonder, that shines so bright.

By simply being himself, he makes my life grand,
A beautiful tapestry, woven by his loving hand.
So here's to my father, my forever hero true,

I celebrate you, and all the wonder you bring to me and
do.

19. Hiraeth

A longing stirs, a yearning deep,
That beckons me to wander, to roam, and to seek,
Pathless woods, where ancient secrets sleep,
And dusty highways, where freedom's spirit creeps.

I catch the scent, of Hiraeth's gentle breeze,
Through long hallways, where memories whisper with
ease,
A bittersweet ache, that echoes through my soul,
A call to return, to a place that makes me whole.

Hiraeth's mystic voice, which whispers low and sweet,
A summons to the heart, to follow where it meets,
The confluence of past, present, and what's yet to be,
A longing that awakens, wild and carefree.

So I'll follow the call, through winding roads and night,
To the place where love and memory, shine with all their
light,

For in the depths of Hiraeth, I'll find my peaceful nest,
A sense of belonging, where my heart can rest.

20. Symphony of the Seasons

Live in each season, as it passes by,
Breathe the air, and let the moments sigh.
Drink the drink, of life's simple delight,
Taste the fruit, of each fleeting night.

Resign yourself, to the earth's gentle sway,
And let the rhythms, of nature guide your way.
Feel the warmth, of summer's sun-kissed skin,
And let the coolness, of autumn's breeze seep in.

Let the snowflakes, of winter's peaceful hush,
Fall gently on your soul, like a lover's gentle rush.
And when spring arrives, with its vibrant display,
Let its colors, and scents, awaken your heart's play.

For in each season, there's a beauty to behold,
A story to be told, of life, and growth, and gold.
So live in each moment, and let the seasons guide,

And you'll find that life's journey, is a path worth
provide.

21. Turbulent minds and Tranquil Tides

On days when worries weigh upon the mind,
And peace seems lost, left far behind,
Remember, dear soul, this wondrous truth:
Sometimes peace is simply breathing deeply, in soothing
truth.

Trust in every inhale, every exhale too,
For in the rhythm of breath, calmness breaks through.
Life's story unfolds, with each passing day,
And in its tapestry, peace will find its way.

The waves of turmoil will crash, as they always do,
But calm waters will also find you, pure and true.
Travel slowly, dear heart, when the journey's steep,
And may peace, in all its forms, be the miracle you keep.

May it find you in the stillness of the night,
In the warmth of love, in the gentle morning light.
May peace, in every shape, be your constant friend,

A beautiful miracle that will never end.